5 EASY ...
DEFEAT THE
OF OVERWHELM

Get a Grip and
Take Back Control of Your Life

By

SUZI LIVINGSTONE

This book is dedicated to anyone who has ever felt the crushing weight of overwhelm, to all those people who felt compelled to carry the world on their shoulders, and especially to those who felt the need to sacrifice their own well-being to ensure the comfort of their families and loved ones.

We have all been there, stunned by the sheer number of things we had to get done, gritting our teeth through the stress, working our way through the physical and mental pressures, because there seemingly was no other option, no better option ...

This book is for you. It was written to reach out to those of you who have ever felt totally defeated before they have even started. This book is meant to extend a lifeline to help you take back control of your life, regain perspective of your priorities, and interrupt the agonizing cycle of overwhelm.

Contents

Introduction

If you've picked up this book then you know what it feels like to be overwhelmed. Daily life demands are endless and you constantly feel on the verge of a mental breakdown. Your boss keeps throwing urgent tasks at you. Your kids need help with a class project. Your dog is destroying the furniture. Your partner is giving you the cold shoulder because you didn't make it to dinner in time -again. To top it all off, you polished off the better part of a family size bag of chips.

You know that you should get organized, move your body, eat a healthy diet, practice self-care, and invest more time in your own well-being. But how can you find the time to do all that when you're already stretched too thin? It seems like each time you finally make the decision to better manage your stress and overwhelm, there's a last-minute commitment that pops up all of a sudden or an urgent crisis that requires your immediate attention. And so you find yourself right where you started.

The truth is, you can't fix overwhelm by adding even more obligations to your to-do list. It rather needs to be undone so you can finally overcome the stress that has caused your mental, emotional, and physical well-being to take a serious hit.

This book provides you with an actionable, step-by-step plan that will allow you to take a step back, understand the root causes of your overwhelm, and work out your priorities accordingly so you can regain control and move forward with your life.

It's a guide that can be used by anyone, whether you're a student, an hourly wage employee, a high-powered executive, or a stay-at-home parent.

This book is not preachy, nor pontificating. It does not offer a litany of quick fixes and short-term solutions. Instead, it will enable you to gain a fresh perspective of your overwhelm and an accurate roadmap to dismantle it.

I'm not one to believe that blind optimism and a delusional vision board are all you need to transform your life and reach wild levels of success. After all, life can be really unpredictable no matter what you do or how thorough of a plan you craft. But with dedication and commitment you will be able to ride the ups and downs of life with a calm and composed attitude.

"Don't let your mind bully your body into believing it must carry the burden of its worries.

– Astrid Alauda

"There is more to life than increasing its speed."

– Mohandas Gandhi

Notes:

Notes:

Notes:

Chapter One

Understand And Assess Your Overwhelm

M any people believe that life-changing events like natural catastrophes, divorce, a terminal diagnosis, or the death of a loved one to be the biggest causes of stress and overwhelm. But what they fail to realize or acknowledge is that the true threat to our physical and emotional well-being is the day in day out overwhelm of present-day life and what it entails. The pace of modern society seems to be ever-accelerating, with one innovation introduced to our daily routines after the other, we're constantly bombarded by products, services, and ideas that claim to be able to increase our efficiency and productivity. We're told from the get-go that downtime is a sin, that our entire value as employees as well as human beings solely resides in the work we do, the contributions we make, and the energy we spend on what other people deem worthwhile. We're condemned for taking time off for ourselves, and we're crucified for indulging in the luxury of self-care practices. We've been conditioned to always ask what's next, to aim for the next level, and never stop because a state of constant motion should be the end goal. We cannot stop, we cannot allow stagnation to creep in. We have to be workaholics, or at the very least aspiring ones. We've been brought up in a world that glorifies overcommitting and overextending ourselves to the point where we're drained of all energy and willpower. So we keep taking on more responsibilities than we can handle, more engagements than we can manage, and more invitations than we can accept, perhaps because we have a hard time saying no, or because we believe that efficiency stems from a packed schedule. Being busy has become a trend in a sense where if you aren't booked 24/7 then you're probably doing something wrong. We have come to this misguiding realization that being successful in this day and age means you have to wake up at 4 a.m. every morning (even on the weekends), go on a run, shower, get some coffee and get to work until it's nighttime and it suddenly dawns on you that between all the snacks and energy drinks, you didn't even have one proper meal all day long. There's no question that, for the most part, our lives have become incredibly complicated, some may say frenetic even. With jam-packed schedules and rampant frustration, free time has become a commodity, a rare occurrence. On the exceptional occasion that we do have some free time, we're ridden with immense guilt because we feel so out of our element. Surely, we could find a 'useful' way to spend our free time. Surely, we cannot allow ourselves to waste time by simply kicking it back and relaxing. Surely, we could be more productive or even get ahead on next week's tasks early on... These are all thoughts that emerge when we keep feeding the cycle of overwhelm because we're unable to sit with our own thoughts and relish in the present moment. We're consumed by this irrepressible urge to keep moving despite how drained, tired, and exhausted we may be. Thousands of books, articles, and posts all based on self-development and continuous improvement get published daily. The self-help section is brimming with 'secrets', 'tips', 'laws', 'habits', and 'strategies' that smart, organized, and highly effective people swear by. We're told to eliminate negative thoughts, ideas, people, and create room for optimism. Then we're told optimism is an illusion that can lead to greater disappointment when the outcome doesn't match our expectations. We're told that it takes 21 days to form a habit, but then it turns out to be 66 days, and other times it takes as long as 254 days. We're told we should have a thorough five-year plan that includes everything we wish to achieve that will get us to the position we want to be in, in five years. Then we're told we should stop obsessing over our future because life is about spontaneity and living in the moment. If we were to actually follow every piece of advice these authors offer, our lives would be in shambles, more overwhelming than ever... The truth is, there is no magical solution that will solve all of your life's problems instantly. There is no ultimate secret that will transform your existence into a happier and more fulfilling one. Everyone is different in their own regard and so one size does not fit all. You can't take a standard formula, apply it to every possible variable, and expect to get the same result each time. What makes one person happy and satisfied may make another person utterly miserable and vice versa. A life free of stress, worries, and anxieties does not come about by not caring at all, nor by choosing reason and logic over sentiments and feelings. Overwhelm is normal, even inevitable sometimes, but suppressing overwhelming feelings and emotions deep into the darkest corners of your mind won't do you any good. What matters the most is how you choose to address overwhelm and not let it take control of your life. The first step in this guide aims to address the root of the problem, and that is identifying why you are overwhelmed in the first place. Most stress catalysts aren't as direct and may be difficult to discern. The thing is, stressors add up over time so your breaking point could occur over the smallest most futile of things. Freaking out over something like a wrinkled shirt, a broken coffee machine, or a dish that sits outside of the sink does not mean you're overly sensitive. It simply means there are many other factors that laid the groundwork for your stress to fester, which led to a sudden outburst at the next thing that didn't align with your idea of what ought to be. When you're swamped and overloaded and you have too much going on yet very little time, you tend to feel overwhelmed. As a result, all of your energy is focused on trying to manage this stress, which keeps you stuck as you never seem to be making any progress. The good news is effective stress management first begins with identifying what is overwhelming you so you can work out a strategy to reduce or eradicate that source. A great way to do this is to make a list of all the situations, challenges, and concerns that incite your overwhelm and trigger your stress response. Take a moment to write down the main issues you are currently facing. You will begin to notice that some of these issues consist of external forces (a number of which you may have no control over), while the rest seem to originate from within.

External sources of overwhelm

External sources of stress and overwhelm include events and situations that happen to you, whether planned or unexpected.

- **Major life changes.** These can be positive, like getting married or having a baby, getting a promotion, or buying a house. But they can also be negative like getting divorced or the death of someone close to you.

- **Unpredictable events.** These include impromptu occurrences such as a sudden increase in rent or having uninvited guests over out of the blue.

- **Environment changes.** Your surroundings may also be a cause of overwhelm, namely a cluttered and messy living space or a cramped work station. A sudden change in the environment, like moving houses or emigrating to a new country can also put a strain on your mental well-being.

- **Workplace stressors.** Common causes of overwhelm at work include an overflowing workload, an endless stream of emails, urgent deadlines, or a demanding boss.

- **Social obligations.** Whether it's meeting new people, going on dates, visiting family, or attending a social event, social obligations can be a major source of overwhelm, especially when you're not the most assertive person and find it difficult to say no or reject another person's invitation.

Managing these external sources of stress and overwhelm is no easy feat, it doesn't happen overnight either. This takes quite a lot of dedication and emotional resiliency in addition to some lifestyle changes -like getting enough sleep, eating healthy, and getting enough physical activity. Not only that but it also entails that you acquire and develop the ability to be more assertive, especially when it comes to your wants and needs. When you consider these external factors you should also take into account how you use your time and energy. The first step is to focus on the things that matter to your the most, reduce unnecessary engagements and activities, and learn to say no to new commitments that aren't of particular interest to you.

Internal sources of overwhelm

Not every overwhelming feeling is an outcome of outside influences. In fact, most of the thoughts that clutter your mind are what trigger your stress response. So overwhelm is often self-induced and a direct result of those ideas and feelings that pop into your head causing frustration, unrest, and turmoil.

- **Fear.** Many people feel overwhelmed because they're paralyzed with fear. Fear of failure, fear of success, fear of the outcome of their decisions, fear of not living up to everybody's expectations, fear of disappointing their loved ones, fear of losing the people close to them, fear that they've taken the wrong path, fear that they don't belong, fear of being forgotten.

- **Lack of control and uncertainty.** Doubt and uncertainty are two of the most common sources of stress, especially for people who like to be in control at all times. Not knowing what might happen next can cause a great deal of anxiety. Anticipation, in many cases, can contribute to growing feelings of overwhelm -for instance waiting for the results of a serious medical test.

- **Beliefs.** These are often attitudes, opinions, behaviors, or expectations, and you may not even be aware of how powerful they are in shaping your experiences. When you set the highest - almost impossible, standards to achieve, you're automatically setting yourself up for overwhelm. Aspiring to accomplish more is a great thing, but it can also be incredibly taxing when the goals become overly ambitious.

The good news is that you have the ability to control your thoughts. The bad news? Your fears and self-limiting beliefs have been your companions for a long, long time, which makes getting rid of them all the more difficult and challenging. With that said, you can still manage these internal sources of overwhelm through reframing your thoughts, adopting a growth mindset, challenging your inner critic, and using mindfulness techniques.

Assignment: Keep a stress journal

Keeping a stress journal for a few weeks is a highly effective stress management tool. Not only will it help you become more aware of the situations in which you're likely to be overwhelmed but it also allows you to understand what triggers those feelings in the first place.

Note down the date, time, and place of each overwhelming situation/episode, then write down what you were doing, who you were with, and how you felt (both physical sensations and emotional experiences). Give each overwhelming situation a rating on a scale of 1 to 10, 1 being mild and 10 being extreme. Use this journal to gain deeper insight into what triggers your stress and how effective you are during those episodes. The point of this assignment is to help you evaluate what causes overwhelm so you can work on developing healthier coping mechanisms.

Take the first step

Recognizing an issue is the first step towards solving it. So, by beginning to understand and assess the roots of your overwhelm, you've taken the initial step in learning to better manage it. The keyword here is 'manage' and not completely eliminate it because stress is an inherent part of daily life and you can only learn effective ways to cope with it and prevent it from taking control over your mind and your surroundings.

"A simple life is not seeing how little we can get by with—that's poverty—but how efficiently we can put first things first.... When you're clear about your purpose and your priorities, you can painlessly discard whatever does not support these, whether it's clutter in your cabinets or commitments on your calendar."

— Victoria Moran

"The idea of balance is a good one, when viewed with two Caveats:

1. *Not everything in our lives deserves the same weight. Aim instead for the correct weight.*
2. *Balance isn't a daily act. Not everything will be given attention every day, and that's ok.*

The difference is in the weight we give things."

— Brooke McAlary

Notes:

Notes:

Suzi Livingstone

Notes:

Chapter Two

Identify Your Priorities

There is no question that all sense of perspective is thrown right out of the window when you're feeling stressed and overwhelmed. As a result, you often find yourself overreacting and allowing small issues to get into your head because you're completely unable to see the bigger picture anymore, and so you've lost all connection with your purpose. Being overextended has become the new norm so much so that your work/life overwhelm is exacerbated by the fact that it takes way too much effort to stay afloat with very few guarantees that the ship will remain sailing in calm waters (if none at all). You probably barely have an unscheduled moment left and the second you set your eyes on your to-do-list, your instincts all but scream for you to run around in utter panic. The truth is, most of the items on your list don't require an immediate response and even if you were to rush things and try to accomplish everything as soon as possible, trying to do too much at once will only affect your ability to be present, your capacity for joy, as well as your effectiveness. When you're looking at numerous tasks all competing for your attention, knowing where to start can be daunting. What you need to ease up your frenetic urgency is to take a step back and identify your priorities. Determining what truly deserves the top spot on your list is how you begin to recognize your limitations and by extension adhere to more realistic expectations. Not only that but when you get to know what your priorities are, you also uncover your 'why', or the reason behind why you do what you do as well as what pushes you to do better and be better. In a way, you become more connected to your sense of purpose and are able to use it as a source of motivation and inspiration when you're feeling down.

Pick your top priorities for now

When you're feeling overwhelmed, it's almost always because you are trying to do way too much all at once. Whether it's by your own volition or whether it's due to tasks piling up, the fact remains that your attention is scattered all over the place and you can't focus on a single assignment because you want to get everything done within a fixed time frame. When this occurs, take a deep breath, and look at everything on your plate to determine your top priorities. What are five things you really want in your life, starting right this moment? What do you want your professional life to look like? Does how you're currently spending your energy fuel your top priorities? Choose 3 to 5 items that you absolutely cannot drop. For most people, these will usually include job responsibilities, children, etc. Your top priorities should consist of things that if you were to abandon, you would be risking relationships, lives, or basic needs like food, clothing, and shelter. You may find that these things only occupy 2 or 3 slots on the top of your list. So if you still have room to add more, whatever you choose to include should be very important to you -working out, reading, playing an instrument, journaling, etc. The critical element here is that whatever you choose as a top priority (that matters to you) should be a task that you couldn't possibly assign to someone else. Now that you have a list of responsibilities, you can move on to making your to-do list. These are the tasks you feel somewhat pressured to do but are not that essential. Rank everything in order of importance so you have a clearer idea of what to tackle first and what can wait. So what do you do with the non-urgent tasks? You can let it sit for a few hours, days, weeks, or months (based on the time window you have) before you decide what to do with them. Allow yourself ample room to let the overwhelm ease before you worry about anything that isn't a priority -even if it's only to decide what to do with it.

Learn to put first things first

The following chart explains the main difference between what is urgent and what is important. You can use it to categorize the different tasks in your daily to-do list. And, yes, something can be urgent all while being unimportant. This entails pointless meetings, make-work assignments, empty conversations, etc. To get out of these, you will most likely have to say 'no' a few times or practice some bold self-advocacy. The urgent and important section is where you get to accomplish those pressing essential tasks (this is the category where your levels of stress and overwhelm are likely to spike). The not urgent yet important category is the golden sector because it allows you to plan for your long-term goals. This also happens to be the most challenging out of the four, namely since it takes a great deal of self-control and self-discipline to stay focused on what you aim to achieve.

	URGENT	**NOT URGENT**
IMPORTANT	**To Do** Important calls, Deadlines, Crises to solve, etc.	**To Plan** Projects, Networking, Quality time w/ loved ones, etc.
NOT IMPORTANT	**To Delegate or Avoid** Pointless meetings, Some emails/calls, etc.	**To Reduce** TV binges, Social media, Mindless distractions, etc.

Identify your knee-jerk reactions

Nailing down the difference between what is urgent and what is a priority can be a struggle, particularly when your thought patterns make the leaps for you. An email detailing an important new project comes in on a busy day and before you know it, your heartbeat is through the roof, you begin to hyperventilate, and your coworker's obnoxious phone call to his dentist is driving you crazy. Between receiving that email and getting all amped up, something happened, and chances are it was the vivid thoughts furiously racing in your mind. The way you react to daily events can either help you in accurately prioritizing those events, or it can send you into a vicious cycle of anxiety and overwhelm. It's hard to embody confidence, reason, and sound judgment when the thoughts in your head have already sent you into a tailspin. With that said, if you want to get out of that frantic state of mind, you need to identify your knee-jerk reactions and thought patterns. So the next time you start to feel overwhelmed, take an inventory of your thoughts. What holds truth to it and what doesn't? To transcend the overwhelm, you need to be able to acknowledge, process, and regulate those knee-jerk reactions that stress can trigger. So in a way, this can inhibit your ability to use language to describe the different aspects of your experience. This is namely because overwhelm is bundled in such a way that it generates an extreme range of emotions, physical sensations, memories, and thoughts within a matter of seconds. When you're overwhelmed, it's essential that you take the time to unpack all the different layers to your knee-jerk reactions and thought patterns so that you can address them individually. Ultimately, this will allow you to slow down the cascade of overwhelming symptoms so you can be more deliberate in your responses. You've likely heard of the expressions *your thoughts become words, your words become actions, your actions become who you are.* Self-talk is, in fact, a big part of who you are, the way you see yourself, and the way you project yourself to those around you. So naturally, when you only focus on being overwhelmed, you're setting yourself up to be just that. You're also inviting even more stress triggers, worries, and anxieties your way. Negativity breeds negativity and when you're deeply entrenched in negative self-talk, it's hard to detach yourself from your thoughts because you see them as an extension of your identity. Imagining a certain action or belief over and over again can have the same effect on your mind and body as if you were to engage in that action or hold that belief. This means if you imagine yourself succeeding, then you are truly more likely to succeed. This is why positive affirmations and visualizations are such a powerful and deeply impactful tool. The thing with visualization, though, is that it can be a double-edged sword. If you dwell in negativity and continue to visualize bad outcomes, you will inadvertently be creating a self-fulfilling prophecy. Instead, try your best to practice more positive self-talk and when feeling overwhelmed, refer to yourself in the second person. This will put you in a mindset that gives you the needed psychological distance all while facilitating self-control and regaining perspective. Stop saying things like "I am too stressed", "I am too overwhelmed", "I won't be able to finish everything in time" ... Instead, talk to yourself like you would to a friend: "Lisa, you are going to find a solution to this problem, I know you can!".

Allow yourself to swing out of balance

There is a lot of hype over constantly doing your best in each and every endeavor. This rising culture that propagates ideals of always giving everything your best is very dangerous, not to say mentally and physically taxing. "Give it your all, give it 100%". "Don't turn in anything that is less than the best you're capable of". "Dare to unlock your full potential at work". "Invest everything you have in the work you do". And so on … And you know what? It's sheer nonsense and it is absolutely ridiculous. Here's the real truth; if you give your all to a project, if you invest 100% every time, then you're going to burn out. You're going to feel drained, exhausted, and unable to carry the simplest of tasks. It's just not realistic, nor possible for that matter. Now I'm not saying you should never try your best or that you should sit around and slack off when it's go-time. What I'm saying, however, is don't be a perfectionist all the time. Don't procrastinate or put things off for an undetermined amount of time because you want to give them more of your energy and attention or because you want to do them perfectly. If your main options are to do nothing or to do something that isn't 100% a reflection of your abilities, then choose the imperfect action over the inaction. This will allow the needle on your stress radar to move instantly. Sometimes, you're presented with more than a single action or inaction, but with many. In those cases, you need to refer back to your list of priorities to decide which part of your life requires your time and energy at that specific moment. So, in this regard, swinging out of balance and favoring one aspect over the other is necessary to maintain equilibrium in your life. When that occurs, give yourself a break, and free your mind from the pressure to keep a perfect balance at all costs. Even when you have your list of priorities perfectly delineated, there will be days when those collide with or overshadow one another - and that's okay.

Suzi Livingstone

Assignment: Your 20-minute life check-up to sort your priorities

To make the most of your day and organize your priorities and responsibilities, ask yourself the following questions.

- **What is in alignment with your goals?**

Take a look at your long-term goals and your to-do list then compare the two. Make sure that you prioritize at least one item that will get you one step closer to your long-term goals. Think of something that your future self will thank you for, even if there are no immediate consequences to not doing it.

- **What will make everything else easier?**

It may be tempting to skip a couple of preliminary steps relating to a project, things like planning and organization. With that said, if you take the time to identify the things that will help make the rest of the process much easier, then you will be giving yourself a good foundation for the remainder of the project.

- **What promotes your own success and happiness?**

Before you consider what, other people want you to do, think of what you can do to promote your own success and happiness. It's essential to acknowledge when you're doing things out of guilt so you can redirect yourself towards the tasks that are most meaningful to your growth as a person in addition to those that are genuinely the best use of your time.

Use this space to write down the top 3 priorities for today (and how you intend to tackle them)

Top 3 for Today
1. _____
_____
2. _____
_____
3. _____
_____

"We all have a million things vying for our attention. If you tell yourself that you don't have enough time to clear out your junk, you might be delaying the well-being and relief you could experience by tackling it. If not now, when?"

— Lisa J. Shultz

"Minimizing forces us to confront our stuff, and our stuff forces us to confront ourselves."

— Joshua Becker

Notes:

Notes:

Notes:

Chapter Three

Organize Your Space And Declutter Your Mind

Whether you're lumbering into the office each morning with your shoulders slumped or you're still working from home, that stack of files you made a mental note to get rid of later may have started to look more like a sagging tower of paperwork that threatens to collapse at any moment instead of the few papers that started it all. A messy office may not seem like a big deal at first, but it can put significant strain on your mental well-being as well as your ability to be productive. When your workspace is all cluttered, it only adds to the noise that your brain has to sort through. Not only that but it could also trigger one of your knee-jerk reactions because of the added stress. Perhaps you're not able to locate crucial files underneath that one giant chaotic pile of trash, or maybe you're sitting uncomfortably trying to push everything to the side so you can fit your laptop on your desk. All of this can add to the existing stress you're currently under. Disarray, lack of prioritizing, and poor organization skills are a surefire recipe for imminent failure. Granted, it's crazy how fast your workspace can go from seemingly organized and tidy to a complete disaster zone. A mere week of hard work and maximum focus can leave your office a cluttered mess. Nevertheless, with proper organization and good decluttering, you can make your workspace a comfortable, functional, and inspiring productivity powerhouse.

Why you should declutter your workspace

A neat and tidy office is more than just a pretty space, it can have tremendous benefits both on the physical and psychological level. While a clean desk isn't always a pre-requisite for unmatched innovation, having a space that is completely free from distractions where everything is quick to find, ready to go, and within reach is definitely a perk.

- **A messy office is overwhelming**

A cluttered space doesn't just affect the aesthetics or reduce the visual appeal but it also affects your mindset. When you're working in a messy office, you may find it difficult to focus and concentrate on the tasks at hand. Because you are distracted by the chaos around you, you will feel a lot more overwhelmed, and every assignment or responsibility you have to fulfill at work will seem insurmountable. The clutter in your workspace adds to the clutter in your mind. The result? Less focus, less energy, less enthusiasm, hence, less done.

- **A clean workspace can increase your productivity**

  Are you feeling flustered and overwhelmed at work? Are you constantly losing track of notes from your meetings, upcoming project plans, and more? Do you feel like you have no idea where anything is on your desk? No, this isn't a corny infomercial to sell you something you don't need but feel compelled to buy because it's 3 in the morning and you haven't gone to bed yet. But it is a friendly push to get you to clean your workspace. We're all trying to get a lot done in very little time. But if you're spending most of your time looking for important items you need, then your productivity levels are bound to take a hit. Not only that but this also puts the needle of your stress radar in a frantic craze. When everything is neatly tucked away and arranged so that each item has its own spot, your hysterical searches will cease, leaving you more time to focus on what matters the most.

- **Tidy surroundings will give you a confidence boost**

A messy workspace also means you have lost or completely misplaced items at some point. Perhaps your manager came by to ask for an important document, and when you went to look for it, it was nowhere to be seen. Even if you did eventually find the document, that distraught search party you initiated at your desk probably didn't put you in the best light with your manager. Wasting time shuffling around your desk, hunting for crucial papers will inevitably add to your frustration. On the other hand, when you can easily produce needed documents without going through a mental breakdown, you will feel a lot more confident. You also won't have to feel/look like you're struggling to get through the day.

- **A clutter-free desk = Improved impressions**

If your boss or manager constantly sees clutter in your workspace, this might change the impression they have of you to an unfavorable one. Having a messy and chaotic desk does not bode well for you because it says to others that you lack basic organizational skills, that you're lazy, careless, inattentive, and neglectful. Based on the look of your office, they might think that you don't care about the job, and if you're a sales representative, they might worry about the impression your workspace will give to potential clients, customers, and businesses with which they want to establish a partnership. However, when your office is all clean and organized, this tells your employers that you're committed to the job, that you respect the workspace, and that you take this position very seriously. When higher-ups in a company or organization feel good about your presence within that establishment, then you can feel even more motivated and dedicated yourself.

- **More space and better comfort**

If sitting at your desk feels more like being trapped in a crowded elevator than it does working at an actual office, then you have way too much stuff laying around. Chances are, you've tried to find a place on your desk for an important file but couldn't find a non-cluttered space. It may even seem like you're trapped in your office with a workstation that is gradually shrinking around you. Consider how difficult it is to complete a task when you're physically uncomfortable and then translate that into this situation. Keeping your desk clean and organized can help make you feel more comfortable and at ease. When you start to clear away all the things you don't need, you will feel a lot more relaxed in this new open space. This can lead to greater comfort and increased productivity.

Declutter your office in 7 simple steps

Now that you're aware of the importance of a clutter-free workstation, you're ready to start organizing your office. This might feel a bit overwhelming at first, but if you stick through with it, I promise it won't be as bad as you think.

- **Step one: remove and recycle**

    The first big step is to clear everything off your desk. This will create more chaos than what you've begun with but it's essential that you have a clear station to work with. Start by tossing away old receipts, post-it notes, pamphlets, etc. Throw all the papers in the recycling bin and anything left can go straight to the garbage. This step might seem obvious, but it's surprising how a phone call or a sudden meeting can distract you from keeping track of what needs to be thrown away

- **Step two: wipe everything down**

    After removing all items from your workspace, grab a bottle of disinfectant, a clean towel, and start wiping everything down. Make sure to get in those nooks and crannies to get rid of all dirt build-up and grime. You will feel much better knowing that all those germs and bacteria are a thing of the past. Don't forget about your computer screen, mouse, and keyboard since those usually tend to collect the most dust. Go over any drawers you have as well as any miscellaneous items like cups, picture frames, plant pots, binders, file organizers, etc.

- **Step three: return what isn't yours**

    Whether your colleague let you borrow a stapler or one of their cables, don't let other people's items take over your office. It's time to get rid of what doesn't belong to you. In an individual pile, sort everything that isn't yours and that you have no immediate use for, then return all the items to their respective owners as soon as possible.

- **Step four: give everything a home**

    For a quick and effective cleaning spree, think less 'each individual item needs a home' and more 'every category of items needs a home'. For instance, all of your in-progress papers can go in one stack, even if those projects aren't necessarily related to one another. You can also chuck smaller containers of office supplies in a nice box or basket. A great way to create more desk space and avoid important files from getting lost or buried under all the clutter is to use a bin to store all the necessary papers. You can label these and put them in different folders based on a system that works best for you and your needs. Use the like-with-like rule as a framework to organize any new additions to your workstation so there's nothing loose left.

- **Step five: go digital**

    Chances are the mess that is taking over your office mainly consists of papers and files. Don't let your filing cabinet turn into a dumpster. Instead, start scanning all of those papers and convert them to easily accessible digital formats. There are many apps that provide services such as project management, business card scanning, cloud storage, and more. This can help you get rid of so much clutter to make more room in your drawers, desk surface, and filing cabinets. With that said, as you digitize files, make sure you do so following a thorough organization system so nothing gets lost.

- **Step six: create an easy-access system**

When you start to put items back in place, whether it's on your desk, in drawers, containers, boxes, and other desk organizing products, make sure you're placing everything with purpose. Establish a proper workflow that enhances efficiency by keeping all the files and tools you use most frequently within reach. They should be close and easy to access. For example, if there's a notebook that you use every single day, then it should be in the very front of your drawer as opposed to a reference file that you only reach out for on some rare occasion. You can even go the extra mile and label everything. Granted, you already know where everything is since you've organized it yourself. But coworkers can use those labels when you're not around to put items back into place.

- **Step seven: commit to regular decluttering**

You got this far and that's great but your decluttering journey does not end here! You have a clean and tidy workstation and you can keep it that way if you stick to regular maintenance and upkeep. Clutter has a way of creeping in on you, and before you know it, you're right back where you started. To avoid external clutter getting inside your head, you need to take action. Commit to frequent decluttering, whether it's 5 minutes a day or an hour on a weekly basis. I recommend that you don't leave clean-ups for Mondays because you want to start your week on the right foot. Instead, do it at the end of the week so you're not met with colossal stacks of paper first thing in the morning when you're back to work.

Are you ready to change your work attitude?

It all starts in your workspace. When you clean and organize your office, you also reorient your mindset towards a more positive state. By decluttering and tidying up your desk, you feel more put together and in control. You're also a lot more productive and creative, hence more likely to get the result you want. An inspiring workstation can do wonders for boosting your mood and raising your spirits. So make sure you implement these tips starting today!

Declutter Your Office Checklist

- o Clear out the top of your desk

- o Empty your cabinet drawers and sort items in like-with-like piles

- o Don't replace anything until all areas have been emptied oud, sorted, and decluttered

- o Wipe everything down including drawers, cabinets, and desk surface

- o Give back what doesn't belong to you

- o Organize the contents of each pile and put those you use the most within reach

- o Use drawer dividers or small boxes to creates different sections in your drawers

- o Use magazine holders and baskets to store items you don't use regularly

- o Establish a daily or weekly routine for resetting your workstation to keep it neat and tidy at all times

5 easy steps to defeat the paralysis of overwhelm

"Time is the most valuable coin in your life. You and you alone will determine how that coin will be spent. Be careful that you do not let other people spend it for you."

— Carl Sandburg

"He who every morning plans the transactions of that day and follows that plan carries a thread that will guide him through the labyrinth of the most busy life."

— Victor Hugo

Notes:

Notes:

Notes:

Chapter Four

Develop Your Time Management Skills

We all tend to spend our day racing against the clock, trying our best to squeeze everything we deem important into those crucial 16 hours (that's considering we get sufficient sleep, which has become a rare commodity, to be honest), whether it's job responsibilities, family obligations, chores, or other urgent tasks. Yet no matter how hard we try, there never seems to be enough time. We've all looked at our huge to-do lists in despair, wondering how are going to complete everything in a timely manner. This can definitely incite one of those knee-jerk reactions that get you all amped up and fretting in a matter of seconds. So before the day has even begun you find yourself stressed and extremely overwhelmed at the number of things you have to accomplish. This is where effective time management skills come in. Knowing how to properly manage your time is essential not only for you to feel more in control and at ease but also for you to have a better idea of the steps to take and the direction your day should be going.

Why is time management important?

I'm sure you've heard of the parable that was circulating the internet back in the early 2000s about the college professor, the jar, the rocks, the pebbles, and the sand. This short anecdote appeared in many forms in all sorts of contexts. But if you don't know the story, allow me to explain the general premise before we get into how this relates to improving your time management skills.

A college professor stood before his class holding an empty jar. He begins to fill the jar to the top with rocks, then he asks the students "is the jar full?", everyone agrees and says that the jar is indeed full. The professor takes small pebbles and adds them to the jar then gives it a good shake so they disperse evenly. Then the professor asks the students once again "is the jar full?". They all agree that it is. Finally, the professor pours sand into the jar, which fills up any remaining space. He asks his students whether the jar is full, they all say yes. One student asks what the point of this demonstration was. Another responds that if you try hard enough, you can always squeeze more things in.

The professor interjects: "no, you need to fit the important things into your life first. Otherwise, the other -secondary- things will take up all the existing space.

The rocks represent the most important things in your life, the pebbles are equivalent to the things that are important but that you could live without, while the sand stands for the remaining 'filler' things.

So how do you effectively divide between rocks, pebbles, and sand, in a way that allows you to spend your time more effectively all while allocating enough time for each aspect of your life? The key is good time management that allows you to work smarter, not harder when doing your tasks.

How to improve your time management skills

The sooner you learn to develop and improve your time management skills, the sooner you can achieve a sense of stability and well-being in your life. You will benefit from a deeper self-understanding, improved productivity, reduced stress and feelings of overwhelm, increased life satisfaction, and healthier relationships with your loved ones. Becoming good at managing the time you have also means you will be less overwhelmed especially because it will allow you to find a way to only accept responsibilities and engagements that you can honor. Moreover, it's also going to provide you with a more functional work/life balance since you will be more aware of when it is time to work and persevere and when it is time to relax and enjoy the company of your friends and family. So here is how you can boost your time management skills in 8 easy steps.

1. Plan your week

Planning your week ahead of time will help you recognize and understand exactly what you need to accomplish during that time so come Monday morning it will take you less time to get into a productive stride. Start your weekly plan on Sundays using a planning method like PPP (Plans - Progress - Problems). Each week set 3 to 5 important plans that you seek to accomplish or that move you towards your long-term goals. When you finish a given 'plan', move it to the 'progress' category. If you encounter any issues, you can move it to 'problems' then begin to brainstorm how you intend to tackle those issues. Implementing a planning methodology will not only help you get an overview of your week but it will also allow you to track your progress as you go.

2. Create a daily to-do list

Use 20 minutes of your morning to compile a daily to-do list that goes along with your weekly plan. This lists all of your priorities for the day in one place. In addition to that, it provides you with a tool to take accountability and keep yourself in check. A detailed to-do list also brings structure into your day, so you're able to get a greater sense of achievement as you're making progress. Schedule demanding or creative tasks that require a fresh perspective at times when you're usually full of motivation and energy, and lower priority tasks for times when you're feeling energetic (for example, when that dreaded afternoon slump settles in).

3. Start your day off with the biggest task

You've probably heard of Brian Tracy's famous 'eat the frog' technique. The frog here is that humongous task that you wake up dreading and that pushes you to procrastinate even further. Ideally, you've already defined this task in the evening or during your weekly plan, though that doesn't make it any easier. Mark Twain said: *"If it's your job to eat a frog, it's best to do it First Thing in the Morning. And if it's your job to eat two frogs, it's best to eat the BIGGEST one first"*. This cuts to the very core of good time management, and that consists of decision, determination, and discipline. When you complete the most unwanted task first thing in the morning, it not only moves it out of your way but it also gives you a tremendous sense of accomplishment and a burst of energy so you feel prepared to tackle anything head on.

4. Set limits for what you'll say yes to

You may want to be accommodating, you may want others to see you as a reliable friend, a loving partner, or a devoted employee, but when you say 'yes' to tasks you have no interest in or things you're not necessarily good at, you're also saying 'no' to other things. For example, taking on a new project or helping a coworker complete their share of the work may entail not seeing your family for dinner or not tucking your kids in bed that night. Accepting every invitation and every assignment might be a way for you to make a positive impression or show your dedication but it also puts a great deal of pressure on your mental and physical well-being. Setting limits to how many things you're inclined to accept from others is essential if you want to reduce overwhelm and improve your time management skills.

5. Take regular breaks

You don't have to be constantly working for you to feel productive. If you're not taking adequate breaks from work, your mindset, as well as your work performance, will begin to suffer. On the other hand, dedicating time in your day to briefly disconnect from your work will allow you to decompress and come back to the tasks at hand with a fresh perspective. Learning when to take a breather will help you develop effective time management so you are able to stress less and accomplish more.

6. Don't multitask

Multitasking is no longer the most desirable skill to have. In fact, nowadays, it's much more valuable to give a single task your undivided attention than it is to try and do too much all at once. This may seem like a time and energy-efficient strategy but the truth is those who focus on doing one thing at a time finish their work much faster than those who simultaneously engage in different endeavors. You lose time when switching from one active task to another and you're also more susceptible to distractions as opposed to choosing quality over quantity.

7. Learn your patterns of productivity

Everybody has distinct patterns of productivity and the amount of energy they have throughout the day. Some people are a lot more efficient in the early hours of the day, while others won't hit the peak of productivity until after lunch or nighttime even. When you determine which parts of the day you tend to get those precious bursts of energy, you can move on to use the time you have more effectively. So during your less productive times, you can schedule those brainless tasks all while ensuring that your 'peak' times are devoted to the bigger and more challenging ones.

Finding the perfect time management strategy requires that you tune in with your productivity patterns but also that you recognize which areas in your life are functional and which ones could use a little work. With only a limited amount of time, it's important that you use your organizational skills to stay focused on the tasks at hand. So use this guide to practice effective time management that will enhance your performance and overall productivity.

Time Management Assignment

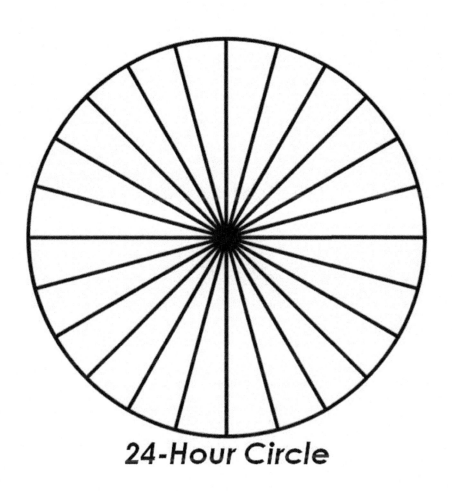

24-Hour Circle

Suzi Livingstone

Use this 24-hour circle to determine how much time you spend on each activity or task (from those listed below). You can also add any items that take some of your time but that aren't part of the list. After you have totaled up everything you can think of, identify how much free time you have.

Activities Breakdown

- ❏ **Reviewing papers**
- ❏ **Working on projects**
- ❏ **Commuting**
- ❏ **Dressing and eating**
- ❏ **Hours of employment**
- ❏ **Responsibilities at home**
- ❏ **Fitness and physical activity**
- ❏ **Phone and computer**
- ❏ **Television**
- ❏ **Entertainment like dating, outings, sports, movies, going out, etc.**
- ❏ **Sleeping**
- ❏ _____
- ❏ _____
- ❏ _____

Total number of hours per week = 168

Subtract your Total _____

Total free hours per week _____

Now that you are aware of how you're spending your time, you need to reflect on your goals and priorities. List your top 10 priorities in order from most to least important.

1. _____

2. _____

3. _____

4. _____

5. _____

6. _____

7. _____

8. _____

9. _____

5 easy steps to defeat the paralysis of overwhelm

How do your Priorities match up to how you spend your time each week?

What do you need to adjust in your weekly schedule to better match your life priorities?

What do you spend time on that you will remove or reduce in your weekly schedule?

"I'm simply saying that there is a way to be sane. I'm saying that you can get rid of all this insanity created by the past in you. Just by being a simple witness of your thought processes. It is simply sitting silently, witnessing the thoughts, passing before you. Just witnessing, not interfering not even judging [...] Because as you become more and more deeply rooted in witnessing, thoughts start disappearing. You are, but the mind is utterly empty. That's the moment of enlightenment. That is the moment that you become for the first time an unconditioned, sane, really free human being."

— Osho

"Certainly work is not always required of a man. There is such a thing as a sacred idleness, the cultivation of which is now fearfully neglected."

— George Mac Donald

Notes:

Notes:

Notes:

Chapter Five

Focus On Your Physical And Mental Well-Being

We spend a lot of time on the go, taking care of kids, maintaining relationships, working full-time jobs, and a thousand other things. Trying to stay on top of everything at all times can be exhausting. Between fulfilling your professional obligations and personal commitments, it seems almost impossible to spare even 20 minutes of your day for yourself. Any free time you have you quickly fill with other responsibilities and activities. So let me ask you this when was the last time you truly rested? When was the last time you detached yourself from everything around you and simply sat and relaxed? I don't mean going to sleep at night or taking a day off work because you were sick. I mean taking the time to sit with your own thoughts and contemplate or just kick back and do the most basic things that give you contentment. If you're constantly stressed out and overwhelmed, chances are you're not taking good care of yourself. You're running against the clock trying to get everything done within a fixed deadline that you seldom have the time to stop and just breathe. But giving yourself a chance to do that is crucial. You can't stay focused, maintain your performance, vigilance, and productivity if you're overly stressed, no matter how much you love your job and no matter how much your loved ones mean to you. Self-care is essential. It's not a luxury only the few lucky ones can afford. It's not an indulgence either despite what many would have you believe. You shouldn't have to feel guilty because you decided to take some time for yourself. You shouldn't have to feel guilty because you're catering to your most basic needs. And you definitely shouldn't have to feel guilty for not giving everything your 100% at all times. You can't give to others what you don't already have. Investing in your physical and mental well-being should be deemed a priority, not an act of permissiveness. Implementing some self-care practices here and there is how you maintain your sanity. Now, I'm not going to ask you to change your entire routine but I'm only going to ask that you allow your body, mind, and soul to breathe. There's this misconception that self-care is about pampering yourself with expensive spa days, which is perhaps why so many people are on the fence about it. Self-care, like the name implies, is about taking care of yourself, spiritually, physically, mentally, emotionally, and socially. It's about eating a healthy balanced diet, drinking enough water, getting enough sleep, meditating, being physically active, etc. Self-care is getting your finances in order and ensuring stability in all aspects of your life. It's knowing when you need a break, whether it be from work, parenting, or just life in general, even if that break is taking 5 minutes off your day to practice mindfulness, to center yourself, or just to step out of a conversation so you don't say something you will regret later. The truth is, you can't expect anybody to push or encourage you to do it. You need to be willing to step up, put yourself first (despite the guilt), and take responsibility for yourself. Because at the end of the day, that's what will give you the strength to keep going and continue to be there for those who need you, no matter how overwhelmed you may be.

Mindfulness and meditation for stress relief

Mindfulness is a very simple, yet incredibly effective form of meditation that allows you to gain control of overwhelming thoughts and behaviors. This is an excellent technique to defuse stress because it enables you to stop jumping from one thought to the next and to stop dwelling on negative ones. Gandhi once said to a group of his followers who asked about his schedule: "I need to set aside one hour each day to meditate". The group was in disbelief. Surely someone as important and busy as Gandhi couldn't afford to spare an entire hour of his day for meditation, and so they told him "there is no way you have that much free time", to which he replied, "well, in that case, I need to set aside two hours a day for meditation". Many people wonder how they will find the time to sit quietly and meditate. What they do not realize is that meditation is one of the few things that is well worth the time investment. The busier you are, the more important it becomes for you to clear your mind if you want to be focused and productive. You don't have to go to the mountains of Nepal to practice mindful meditation. Nor do you have to join a weekend retreat and take a vow of silence. The beauty of meditation is that you can practice it anytime and anywhere. Mindful meditation is a simple act that allows you to bring all of your attention to the present. So you get to observe your thoughts clearly and objectively without any judgment. This way, you learn to live in the moment so your life doesn't pass you by. This may sound too abstract for you, or perhaps even too complicated if you're new to mindfulness and meditation, but it isn't. Anybody can do it, even with the busiest of schedules. You just have to be willing to give it a chance.

Quick 5-minute meditation for when you're short on time

One of the most valuable aspects of meditation is that it can help you build resilience over time. It can teach you how to respond to challenging times in your life from a relaxed and mindful place rather than reacting out of fear and overwhelm. Moreover, it can help you let go of negative thoughts, feelings, and behaviors that do not serve you. You can redirect your mind away from pointless ruminations with frequent practice. To get started, just five minutes of meditation has the power to bring quick and efficient stress relief. So whether you're new to this practice or you want to try a quick session, here's how to implement a 5-minute meditation into your day.

1. Find a distraction-free zone

To get started, you need to find your meditation spot. Ideally, this should be private and free from external disturbances. You can do this in your bedroom, living room, or even backyard, as long as you feel safe, comfortable, and at ease in that space. Once you've picked your meditation spot, make sure it's not messy or cluttered. Quickly clean around for a bit before you get settled.

2. Set a timer

Now that you have your meditation space ready, make sure to set a timer for 5 minutes so you don't end up missing any calls, appointments, or meetings. You can use your phone's default timer or download a meditation app to keep track of your progress. If you prefer to have something in the background, you can also put some meditation music on to help you get in that zen state of mind a bit faster.

3. Relax your body

When it's time to begin, close your eyes, relax your body, and focus on your breathing. Take a few deep breaths from your diaphragm, and as you exhale, release the tension in your body. Focus on a five-second count as you breathe. Slowly inhale from the belly, move the air into your ribs and chest, and hold it for the fifth count. Feel the air travel down your windpipe and into your lungs. Then feel your body shift as you exhale pushing the air out of your lungs.

4. Focus your mind

Freeing your mind of all interruptive ideas can seem impossible at first. When you're too caught up in trying to eliminate each and every germinating thought is rather counterintuitive. Instead of 'thinking of nothing', focus your mind on the state of being Don't worry if you get intrusive thoughts that take your attention from breathing. Simply observe the thoughts, acknowledge them, and let them pass then shift your focus back to your breathing. After some practice, you will be able to fully immerse yourself in the act of breathing at the expense of every other thought. When you accept that bringing your mind to the present *is* the meditation, you'll find it much easier to keep your mind still.

5. Repeat positive affirmations

The main goal of mindful meditation is to put the stream of thoughts racing through your mind on hold. A great way to do this is to choose a short positive affirmation about yourself and repeat it over and over again each time you inhale and exhale. One potent phrase of choice is "I am capable". Not only is it simple enough to keep you grounded but it will also stop other thoughts from taking over.

Interrupt the cycle of overwhelm

Any moment when you find yourself stressed, overwhelmed, and stuck is the perfect opportunity to practice mindful meditation. Stop everything you're doing and allow yourself a quick 5-minute session to focus on your breathing. Let the swarm of thoughts dissipate as you repeat your favorite affirmation and you'll be surprised how grounded and in control, you will feel once the session is over.

Notes:

Notes:

Notes:

Conclusion

The purpose of this book was to introduce you to the 5 fundamental steps that will allow you to conquer overwhelm and stay ahead of the curve.

Step 1 is about evaluating your stress and identifying its root causes. This initial part is crucial because it lays the groundwork for what comes next. If you don't know what it is in your life that is causing you tremendous overwhelm, then how can you expect yourself to overcome this pressure?

Step 2 is about learning the art of prioritization. Sometimes, we tend to get lost under the monstrous tasks in our to-do lists. The cumulative effect of responsibilities, engagements, and commitments may cause us to lose perspective of the things that really matter in life. And without a clear sense of purpose, anxiety and doubt begin to gradually creep up on you, making you question your every thought and action. The best way to remedy what sometimes seems to be an unsolvable is to reflect on the things we have to do that fulfill our basic needs, the things that push us to do our best but also the things that bring meaning to our lives.

Step 3 is about the power of a clean, tidy, and organized workspace. When all you can see is clutter and chaos, that mess in your surroundings tends to shift to your mindset as well. Maintaining a clutter-free environment is a key element in increasing productivity and reducing stress.

Step 4 focuses on the importance of time management, not just as a skill, but as a lifestyle choice too. The truth is, that stress and overwhelm are often the product of a poorly managed schedule where you overestimate your abilities and set impossible expectations for yourself. So learning how to better manage your time, through establishing balanced routines and schedules is vital to alleviate the pressures of uncertainty and provide yourself with a healthy equilibrium of work and leisure.

Step 5 focuses on the physical and mental aspects of your well-being. This final step aims to introduce you (the reader) to healthier coping mechanisms that will allow you to better handle your feelings of overwhelm without resorting to quick fixes or toxic behavior. Mindfulness, meditation, and positive affirmations, being some of the most notable relaxation techniques. Taking better care of yourself and working on improving your mental and physical well-being will not only replenish your energy but it will also help you center yourself and stay grounded when the going gets tough.

Now that you can successfully move your mind to the other side of stress and overwhelm, it doesn't mean that it will always be easy, but it does mean that you have the skills and tools to work with what you've got and improve the situation you're in. You won't magically have more time to accomplish what you've set out to do but you will have more energy to tend to your priorities and fulfill your responsibilities. With this renewed sense of control and perspective, you can feel confident in your ability to handle even the most stressful of situations. And with your improved sense of prioritization, you can begin to invest more time in the things you've always wanted to try, the people you've always wanted to get to know better, and the communities you've always wanted to give more to. Everything that you've put on hold for the longest time is no longer impossible or insurmountable. You are in the driving seat.

you have the power to decide how your day goes by and how your time is spent.

Only you can decide how best to live your life and only you can choose who you want to be and how you want to be seen.

So, choose well!

Notes:

Notes:

Notes:

Bibliography

Links

https://www.skillsyouneed.com/ps/stress-tips.html

https://heartmdinstitute.com/stress-relief/6-powerful-ways-defuse-effects-stress/

https://greatergood.berkeley.edu/article/item/four_ways_to_calm_your_mind_in_stressful_times

https://www.forbes.com/sites/ashleystahl/2020/02/25/5-steps-to-release-overwhelm-from-your-life/?sh=533f9ac46f26

https://wendymillermeditation.medium.com/5-steps-to-basic-self-care-when-life-overwhelms-you-ee8a8954b590

https://www.lifehack.org/articles/productivity/stop-limiting-beliefs-and-take-back-your-life.html

https://www.refinedroomsllc.com/home-office-declutter-things-to-toss/

https://figarigroup.com/blog/how-declutter-office-space-increase-productivity/

https://www.mindtools.com/pages/article/newHTE_00.htm#:~:text=Time%20Management%20Definition,tight%20and%20pressures%20are%20high.

https://www.entrepreneur.com/article/299336

https://www.liquidplanner.com/blog/7-essential-time-management-strategies/

https://www.nhs.uk/oneyou/every-mind-matters/top-tips-to-improve-your-mental-wellbeing/

https://uhs.umich.edu/tenthings

https://www.mayoclinic.org/tests-procedures/meditation/in-depth/meditation/art-20045858

https://www.nytimes.com/guides/well/how-to-meditate#:~:text=Mindfulness%20meditation%20is%20the%20practice%20of%20actually%20being%20present%20in,present%20moment%20without%20any%20judgment.

Books

Less Doing, More Living: Make Everything in Life Easier - Ari Meisel

Stress Less. Achieve More.: Simple Ways to Turn Pressure into a Positive Force in Your Life - Aimee Bernstein M. ED MFCC

Stress Less, Accomplish More: Meditation for Extraordinary Performance - Emily Fletcher

The Joy of Being: Supporting hardworking mums to stress less & live more - Marina Pearson

The Stress Management Handbook A Practical Guide to Staying Calm, Keeping Cool, and Avoiding Blow-Ups.

Eva Selhub, MD

The Wellbeing Workout: How to manage stress and develop resilience - Rick Hughes, Andrew Kinder, Cary L. Cooper

101 Ways to Make Every Second Count: Time Management Tips and Techniques for More Success with Less Stress - Robert W. Bly

The Mindfulness Workbook for Anxiety The 8-Week Solution to Help You Manage Anxiety, Worry & Stress

Tanya J. Peterson, Ms, NCC

About The Author

Suzi Livingstone

Suzi is a busy mom of two. She works part-time and between her responsibilities at work and her homelife, Suzi manages a very engaged schedule.

She has always been interested in achieving a healthier and more balanced lifestyle that would allow her and her family to thrive. Because she leads such a busy lifestyle, she likes simple yet efficient solutions that she can easily incorporate into her life that will benefit her whole family.

Like many working moms in her position, Suzi has often felt overwhelmed and paralyzed by the sheer weight of things that she has had to manage. And like many, she doesn't have the time to read detailed manuals and elaborate self-help books that involve intricate steps and complex processes. She appreciates the simplicity of a quick step by step guide that aims to demystify a subject and give a no nonsense, practical approach. Preferably one that includes lots of helpful tips and best practice advice that anyone can implement into their busy schedule to stress less and accomplish more. In other words, a comprehensive guide that can help her regain control of her life, which is why she has approached this book in the same way.

Printed in Great Britain
by Amazon

37010118R00066